BRUNO
THE BRAVE
BUNNY

Written by:
Courtney Rombs

In a meadow, warm and wide,
little Bruno liked to hide.

He dreamed of hopping,
high and free, but thought,
"that's not for a shy bunny like me."

He saw the birds fly through the sky,
and wished that he could hop so high.

He saw the squirrels climb tree by tree,
and sighed, "that's far too tall for me."

Bruno's heart was small and shy,
afraid to jump, afraid to try

First came Tilly, turtle slow,
who smiled and said, "give it a go!"

"Start with one hop, small and light.
You'll land just fine—it'll be all right!"

But deep inside, he heard a cheer,
"be brave, be bold,
there's nothing to fear!"

So Bruno wiggled, twitched his nose, bent his knees, and up he rose!

A tiny hop, just off the ground,
and oh! His heart began to pound.

"I did it!" Bruno gave a cheer,
though his legs still shook with fear.

"It wasn't big, it wasn't high,
but I was brave enough to try!"

And with each hop, he felt so strong,
"maybe I've been brave all along!"

Soon he was hopping here and there,
leaping high without a care.

He learned that courage starts inside,
and grows each time you try, not hide.

And from that day, Bruno would say, "I'm brave in my own bunny way!"